NAOMI

When I Feel Worthless, God Says I'm

Enough

STUDY GUIDE | FOUR SESSIONS

Kasey Van Norman, Jada Edwards,
Nicole Johnson

With Karen Lee-Thorp

ZONDERVAN®

ZONDERVAN

Known by Name: Naomi
Copyright © 2019 by Kasey Van Norman, Jada Edwards, and Nicole Johnson

This title is also available as a Zondervan ebook.

Requests for information should be addressed to:
Zondervan, *3900 Sparks Dr. SE, Grand Rapids, Michigan 49546*

ISBN 978-0-310-09657-3

Cover image: © LanaBrest/Shutterstock
Interior design: Denise Froehlich

First Printing November 2018 / Printed in the United States of America

Contents

How This Study Works

5

Session 1
When Hard Times Hit

11

Session 2
Behind the Scenes

37

Session 3
Better than Being Fixed

57

Session 4
From Bitter to Blessed

77

About the Authors

96

How This Study
Works

Naomi: Down, Maybe—But Not Out

Loss. Grief. Trauma. Seclusion. Most of us have experienced one or more of these to some degree. How do we thrive in difficult times without being overcome by bitterness? There's a woman in the Bible who faced that question, struggled with it, experienced a whole range of emotions, and eventually took the action she felt she needed to take to get to the other side of her broken down, bitter self. Her name is Naomi. Can you relate? Have you been there too?

When we first meet Naomi, she is fully wallowing in her victim status. Her heart is exposed and raw to the touch. She has lost everything that made her life worth living: her husband, both of her sons, her home. Broke and with no source of income, she is facing an unknown future. But with the help of her daughter-in-law Ruth, who is a widow too, Naomi starts to make choices that give God room to work behind the scenes on her behalf. Her life starts to change.

We see through Naomi's story that when we go through heartbreak and loss, and we're just "so done," God is not done. He can and will redeem everything in our lives. Through her story we can learn to go beyond platitudes about trusting God into a place where trust makes sense to us, and faith is a more natural by-product of our pain.

Naomi: When I Feel Worthless, God Says I'm Enough is a study for women who want to get into the real, messy parts of our lives that are usually under wraps. Through each video session, we will engage with a Bible teacher, a Christian counselor, and an actor portraying present-day scenarios. These leaders will help us explore the human perspective of Naomi: how she felt, how she saw herself, and how others saw her. They will also show us how we can all relate to aspects of Naomi and her story. We will discover God's perspective: how God sees Naomi and how God sees us. Through these perspectives, we will find our own stories in the pages of Scripture.

A Typical Session

A session of the study will go like this:

Check In. In Session 1 you'll introduce yourselves. In later sessions you'll have a chance to share something you discovered about yourself in-between sessions.

At a Glance: Naomi. This is a quick snapshot of an age-old problem we still deal with today, Naomi's age-old solution or mistake, and a taste of God's wisdom on the subject.

Watch The Video. Each video segment is 20–25 minutes long. It opens with a drama and then moves into a fast-paced teaching. Session 1 begins with all three of the presenters together, talking about the theme of the series. This study guide contains space for you to take notes on what you see in the video.

Group Discussion. The heart of the study is your conversation with the other women in your group. You'll be talking mainly about the real experiences of your lives. However, because this isn't group therapy, we strongly recommend that you commit yourself to the group ground rules discussed below.

Closing Prayer. End with your group leader or a volunteer reading aloud the prayer suggested in this section. Of course, any offered prayer is acceptable.

Keep This Close. These are a few short, memorable lines from the video that you may want to copy into your phone to go back to during the week.

On Your Own. Finally, you'll find five or six activities you can select from to carry your exploration of the topic deeper during the week. There is one verse of Scripture you can memorize and come back to over the remaining sessions of the study. There are journaling ideas. You can read Naomi's story in the Bible. You can pray or reflect on the drama. Do whichever of these activities you find helpful. Don't feel pressure to do more than you have time for. You'll have a chance to share something you got out of these activities when your group gathers next time. You'll also have a chance to recite your memory verse together.

Group Ground Rules

This study gives you more of an opportunity to open up about your real life than most studies. You won't be pushed, but you will be invited, to talk about how you see yourself and how you live. But your group is not a therapy session. It's not led by a counselor. If you need professional counseling or a forum to share the story of your past, ask your group leader or church leaders to recommend resources.

The following ground rules will help you stay on track. You should go over them in your first meeting to be sure that everyone understands and agrees.

Confidentiality. Everything shared in the group must stay in the group. Don't repeat to outsiders what others share, even if you are all friends. If a group member misses a meeting, don't bring her up to date by sharing what others said in her absence. If something happens in the group that upsets you, don't discuss it with someone outside your group. Go to your group leader.

Disclosure. This should be a safe place to tell the group the difficult truths of your past. However, the group does not need all the ugly details. Give your group the four-or five-sentence summary of your situation. If you need someone to hear the whole story, ask your group leader to help you get connected with a counselor. She can help you find the person on your church staff who has the names of counselors in your area.

Tears. It's often good to cry when you share something hard. You're not embarrassing the group. If someone in your group cries, avoid words and actions that attempt to fix her sadness or solve her problem. Comfort is good; fixing is not. Don't let tears derail your time together. Keep going. The woman who has tears will be better sooner if the conversation carries on.

Shared Airtime. Everyone in the group needs an equal chance to talk. Avoid telling long stories, especially about your past or about what you are struggling with today. If you have a lot on your mind that needs to be said, ask your group leader to help you get connected with a counselor.

Present Orientation. Naomi's past will come up in the study, and you'll have some time to think about your past. But for group discussion, concentrate on talking about who you are today, shaped by your past, but not living in the past. Don't ask the group to sit through an account of what you went through. That's for counseling.

Advice. Avoid giving advice to other group members. If someone reveals a problem she is having and doesn't seem to know what to do about it, it can be tempting to suggest solutions. Avoid doing this. You can give her the gift of listening to her and accepting her as she is, and you can pray for her later on your own. Likewise, you should avoid asking the group to suggest solutions for situations you are facing. If you feel out of control and need help, ask your group leader to help you find a counselor.

What Materials Are Needed for a Successful Group?

- → Television monitor or screen
- → DVD player
- → Four-session DVD
- → One study guide for each group member (you will be writing in the study guide, so you will each need a copy)
- → Bible(s) (at least one for the group, but encourage all members to bring their Bibles)
- → Pen or pencil for each person

When Hard Times hit

In chaos,
GOD is our
constant.

Times of misery are inevitable in this life. Even in our society, with its advanced medical science, people still suffer and die. Sometimes death hits unexpectedly. Sometimes an illness persists for years with surgeries, treatments, symptoms, and perhaps the worst: uncertainty.

Other losses can be just as devastating: unemployment, divorce, rebelling children, unexpected expenses, substance abuse, disability, incarceration—the possibilities are endless. Such losses make us feel like we're wading through mud in an unknown territory and can't get our bearings. If you haven't yet experienced something that feels like a huge loss, you're probably familiar with smaller ones that can sting just as badly in the moment.

Have you felt like God is silent in these times? We wonder how he could allow such disasters. If God is so powerful and so good, why doesn't he change our circumstances or find a way to end our suffering? It's the age-old question, "Why does a good God allow bad things to happen?" But the truth is that in this broken world, in his sovereignty and grace, he allows suffering to afflict lots of people every day because he knows the end of the story—the good and perfect and whole end.

In this study we're going to be introduced to a woman named Naomi who lost her husband and both of her sons to death. She was so distraught she tried to change her name to "Bitter." But through a strange, yet sovereign, turn of events, Naomi found a way of dealing with her suffering without giving up her commitment to a God who was real and good. It took time. Things didn't get better overnight. But she found a way forward and went for it. She didn't stay stuck.

Check In

Welcome to the first session of *Naomi: When I Feel Worthless, God Says I'm Enough*. To get started, give everyone a chance to do the following:

→ Say your name, unless everyone in the group knows you. Then, share just three or four sentences about something or someone you've lost or some experience that has left you feeling worthless.

Take a minute on your own and write down your response to these questions (you won't have to share your answers):

→ Think of your emotional and spiritual life like your gas tank. On a scale of 0 to 5, with 0 being empty and 5 being full, how full is your tank today? Mark where you are on the measuring line below.

0	1	2	3	4	5
empty					full

→ If your tank is not very full, how much *hope* do you have of its being full one day in the future? Can you look forward to a day when things will be a lot better than they are now, or do you see emptiness as far as the horizon? Mark your level of hope on the measuring line below.

0	1	2	3	4	5
no hope					lots of hope

Where in Scripture: Ruth 1-4

Age-old problem: Loss and grief

Age-old mistake: Blaming God

God's timeless wisdom: Give voice to the depth of your pain, and keep trusting God at the same time. Consider how the Psalmist claims his pain and struggle. He is honest about his frustration with God's lack of response — or so he thinks. He is basically calling God to the carpet but then it's as if he remembers or recalls just who it is he is calling out to — God. Just a momentary lapse of reverence for who God is keeps us from trusting what he is capable of. *"O my God, I cry by day, but you do not answer, and by night, but I find no rest. Yet you are holy, enthroned on the praises of Israel"* *(Psalm 22:2–3 ESV).*

Video Notes

Play the video segment for Session 1. It's about 26 minutes long, and you will be introduced to three speakers. As you watch, use the following outline to record thoughts that stand out to you.

DRAMA: Nicole

An art teacher moved cross-country after a divorce, and when she opened the boxes, everything was broken. Was God punishing her for ending her marriage?

TEACHING: Jada

Sometimes God will allow pain in your life to push you out of a place you shouldn't have been in to begin with.

In her hardest time, Naomi is still representing God well.

Does your life, even when it doesn't feel great, still make someone else want to choose God?

TEACHING: *Kasey*

A trauma to your brain is any time the experience is greater than your reality.

Let yourself lament. To lament is just to say out loud what you feel.

Pain is God's way of preparing us for our purpose and revealing his promise.

GOD doesn't buy our affections with *blessings*.

Leader, read each numbered prompt to the group.

1 What stood out to you most from the video?

2 Kasey talked about lament. When we lament, we put words to the deep, internal grief we feel over the loss of something significant. How hard is it for you to lament? Have you ever allowed yourself to speak or write about your deepest feelings of sadness, loss, loneliness, fear, etc.?

3 Have you received help from believing Christians in painful past seasons? What feeling triggers at the thought of trusting Christian people with your pain?

4 Jada said God sometimes uses pain to push us out of a place that isn't good for us. What are some examples of situations that God might want to push us out of? How might pain be the thing that gets us out of those situations?

5 Naomi modeled faith in God so well that her daughter-in-law Ruth decided to abandon her culture and go with Naomi to follow this God. Think of the people who have modeled faith in God to you. What have they said, done, and been that has made God attractive or compelling?

6 Why do you suppose people often distance themselves from God when life gets hard? What assumptions about God and suffering does this distancing reflect?

Some people think God exists to make them happy. They commit to him with the expectation that he will bless their health, their loved ones, their job, and everything else in their world. Yet, when he allows something to go horribly wrong, they feel betrayed.

While it's true that God does involve himself in our lives and that he will empower us to make good choices, he isn't necessarily interested in making sure our lives go smoothly according to our standards. Like a loving parent, God is much more interested in helping us become strong in character, loving toward others, and trusting toward him. Because we live in a world riddled with sin, he often allows us to endure terrible losses without giving us reasons why. Suffering happens to other people; why not to us? God doesn't buy our affections with blessings. He wants us to love him for himself regardless of our losses. Jesus is God in the flesh, and he came to earth and suffered horribly, partly so that we would know that he knows exactly what it's like to be human in a broken world. He understands what we're going through, and he's right here with us.

1 What reasons do we have for staying faithful to God even when life is really hard?

8 How do you respond to the idea that if you're going through a dark season, you need to go to your local church and surround yourself with people who know God? How helpful does that sound to you, and why?

In preparation for the coming week, write one thing you want to gain from your study time:

(ex.: hope for my future, a better understanding of who I am ...):

Closing Prayer

Ask for a volunteer to read this prayer aloud:

Jesus, you know all the intimate details of the losses each one of us has suffered. You have allowed us to suffer in many ways with many unanswered questions. And yet we know that you are good and you hold our good in your heart. We also know that you have been on earth where we are and endured worse suffering than we can imagine. You know what it's like to be betrayed. You know what it's like to lose loved ones to death. You know what terrible physical suffering is like. You willingly endured the burden of the sin of every person on earth and the feeling of your Father's absence that this involved. And you are with us now in the midst of what we're going through. Please strengthen us to hold onto our faith and empower us to make good decisions. Help us to trust you, even when we can't see the future. Please go with us, and lead us to the other side of what we're going through. In your name we pray, amen.

Keep This Close

As you go on your way this week, here are some thoughts from the video that you may want to save in your phone or write on a sticky note so you can refer back to them:

→ Does your life, even when it's not great, still make someone want to choose God?

→ When life is chaotic, God is your center point.

→ Let yourself lament with the people who know your real name.

On Your Own

Each session of this study also includes activities you can do each day between group meetings. These will help you work through and into a deeper understanding of both the Bible and how it relates to your personal life. **Don't feel you need to do all of these activities. Choose those that are helpful to you. The goal is to grow and develop a stronger relationship with God.** There will be time at the beginning of your next meeting to share whatever you've learned from these activities.

There are many good techniques that may help you memorize Bible verses. Here are some of them:

1. *Write out the verse by hand on paper, along with its reference (in this case, Psalm 81:10). We remember as much as 80 percent more of what we write by hand than what we type electronically. That's because handwriting stimulates a more helpful part of the brain than typing does.*

2. *Even better, hand write the verse and reference five times.*

3. *Read the verse aloud and act it out in an exaggerated way. Proclaim it dramatically. Actors have learned that the dramatic use of your body and voice will create associations in your brain.*

4. *Go for a walk and recite the verse and reference aloud. Walking increases memory formation.*

5. *Copy the verse and reference into your phone or onto a card you can keep with you.*

6. *Return to the verse three times a day to rehearse it. Say it aloud. Do this for all four weeks of this study.*

Learning the verse with its reference will help you find it in the Bible if you want to read the larger story around the verse.

Memory Verse

One thing we really hope you'll do is memorize a verse of the Bible. Committing verses to memory enables you to deeply internalize their truth and to have them with you when you need them. Here is the memory verse for this study:

> *I am the L*ORD *your God,*
>
> *who brought you up out of Egypt.*
>
> *Open wide your mouth and I will fill it.*
>
> (PSALM 81:10 NIV)

The point of this verse is that Naomi starts the story empty (Ruth 1:21), but she will end it full. So will we.

The psalmist is reminding his listeners of the way God rescued and provided for their ancestors. When their ancestors were slaves in Egypt, God did miracles to free them and bring them into a land of their own. God wants to provide for us in the same way. All we need to do, he says in verse 9, is to keep from bowing down to other gods. There are so many other tempting gods we could worship, like comfort, or money, control, sex, relationships, drugs. But all of these, if we make gods of them, will let us down. God pleads with us to believe his promise that he will provide for us if we worship only him. You'll have a chance to discuss this promise further in Session 2.

DRAMA ACTIVITY: Broken, Part 1

The drama was about an art teacher who moved across the country after a divorce. When she opened the moving boxes, everything was broken. She wondered: was God punishing her for ending her marriage? But then she remembered that God knew how hard she had tried to save her marriage. Still, though, when she looked at all the broken pieces of her life, she couldn't help thinking, *I wish I could fit in one of those boxes and just get thrown away.*

1 Have you ever wondered if God was punishing you? If so, what led you to wonder that?

Jesus took on himself the punishment we deserve (Romans 5:6–11). God doesn't send suffering on us to punish us; he allows it to remind us of who we really are. Jesus is in the fire with us—experiencing the flames with us. He mourns with us, hurts over our sufferings with us, and celebrates our victories with us. The hotter the flames burn, the closer he gets (Isaiah 43:2). Suffering shows our faith is genuine. It is being tested as fire tests and purifies gold *"so that the tested genuineness of your faith . . . may be found to result in praise and glory and honor at the revelation of Jesus Christ" (1 Peter 1:7 ESV).*

2 Have you ever felt something like, "I wish I could fit in one
   of those boxes and just get thrown away"? Who is God to
   you when you are feeling like that? Is God someone you
   move toward or away from in a situation like that? Why?

3 Read Psalm 88. This is a psalm of lament. There are lots of
   psalms of lament in the book of Psalms, because the Jews
   thought that lament was important for individuals and for the
   gathered community of God's people. Which statements of
   lament in this psalm are especially meaningful for you?

4 How would you describe this psalmist's attitude toward
   God? What does he say *to* God and *about* God? Does he
   move toward or away from God?

5 Does the psalmist feel better by the end of the psalm?
What does this say to you about the process of lament?
About God's view of people who are lamenting?

6 Many psalms of lament contain expressions of trust in
God and/or shouts of praise to God that he will deliver
us. But this one doesn't. Why do you suppose a hundred
percent lament is included in the Bible?

Coping with Loss

TEACHING ACTIVITY

In the video, Kasey named two effective ways to deal with loss and suffering: lament (on your own and with others) and spending time with God's people, who will help you stay pointed toward God. There are lots of other ways people try to deal with loss—some of them are constructive, and some are destructive. In this exercise, you'll have a chance to reflect on how you currently handle loss and what you want to do in the future.

1   First, describe the *feelings* and *thoughts* you are having in a season of loss or suffering. Feelings are things like anger, sadness, fear, joy, confusion, and numbness. If you're not sure what you feel, try probing around and putting words to it. You may be feeling several things. You may be feeling numb because your coping strategies are designed to tamp down unpleasant feelings. Complete these sentence starters and use the additional space if necessary.

I feel _____ .

I feel like _____ .

I want to _____ .

I wish _____ .

I'm hungry for _____ .

I think _____ .

God seems like _____ .

2   What are some of the things you have done to try to cope with loss or suffering? List as many as you can think of. For example, maybe you eat, post or read on social media, get together with a friend, crawl into a cave, and so on.

3   Which of these coping strategies have been truly helpful?

4   Looking back, which strategies have been less than helpful, or downright harmful?

5   Do you seek numbness, an absence of negative feelings? If so, do you believe it's moving you forward? Explain.

Make an appointment with a friend to share your lament with her. Ask her if it's okay if you just pour out your heart uncensored about what you're going through. Don't have a friend you can talk to like that? Ask God to reveal her to you, because he promises she is there. Until then, consider talking with a professional counselor. Your group leader may be able to help you connect with one.

Naomi in the Bible

SCRIPTURE ACTIVITY

Look up Ruth chapter 1 in your Bible and read it.

This story takes place many centuries before the time of Jesus, when the nation of Israel was just getting started. Israel had not yet had a king. Instead, various parts of the country were ruled by people called judges (verse 1).

1   In both Moab and Israel at that time, there were few opportunities for women to work outside the home. Most women were supported by their male relatives. A widow without sons was looking at poverty. How do you think this fact influences what Naomi says and does in this chapter?

2 We aren't told why Ruth doesn't go home to her family and live with them until she can find another husband. What possible reasons can you think of?

3 What do you learn about Ruth's relationship with Naomi from what Ruth says in verses 16-17? What do her words suggest about each woman?

4 Have you ever been committed to someone like that? Have you ever had someone commit to you like that? If so, how has that commitment affected your life? What thoughts and feelings go through your mind when you think about Ruth's commitment?

5　In verse 20 Naomi says, "Don't call me Naomi," which means *pleasant*. Instead, she says, "Call me Mara, which means *bitter*, because the Almighty has made my life very bitter." To what extent do you think God is responsible for the bitterness of her life? Why?

6　What is your personal takeaway from this chapter of Ruth?

Journal Time

If you are going through something painful or are trying to come to terms with past suffering, it can be enormously helpful to pour out your thoughts and feelings on paper. You don't have to write it so that somebody else understands it; you just put down what's in you however it comes out. You don't have to share any of it if you don't want to.

Choose *one* of the following topics to journal about:

→ Have you ever felt like God had turned against you? Do you feel like that now? If so, describe the situation that is making you feel that way, and describe what you are feeling toward God. It's okay to say exactly what you feel, even if you're angry at God.

→ Has God ever used pain to push you out of a place where you didn't need to be? If so, describe the place you were in and how God worked in your life to move you to a better place. Focus on how he used pain to motivate you. If you're in the situation right now, and you feel like God is trying to use pain to push you out of it, describe where you are and what better place you might go to.

→ What is the loss or hardship you are currently struggling with? Describe what you're going through and the feelings you're having. If there's a history to it and it will help you to lay out the history, include that. If you have questions about what you should do, write those down.

Whichever topic(s) you choose, finish up by writing about this question: What will you do differently in your day-to-day life as a result of this reflection? Use extra paper if necessary.

Listening

PRAYER ACTIVITY

For many of us, thoughts buzz around in our heads like flies, hard to capture and harder to quiet. For others, we have no idea what the thoughts in our heads do, because we're distracted all day long with people, tasks, entertainment, phone notifications, and social media. Our attention span is shorter than our pinky nail, and we feel comfortable only when something is occupying our attention.

God, however, seems to speak in the quiet. His voice is soft and low, so we don't hear him unless we're paying our full attention for a period of time. Giving our full attention is a skill that takes practice. We have to choose to slow down and endure the silence. At first, the silence can be uncomfortable. Thoughts and feelings arise that we might not want to deal with. Our minds run off on rabbit trails. We itch to grab our phones. However, if we persist in offering our stray thoughts to him, and settle back to listen, eventually we can learn to listen.

Take some time now to allow God the opportunity to speak to you. Find a quiet place where you can be alone. Turn off your phone—or better still, leave it somewhere else so it doesn't draw your eye and your thoughts. Lay before him your thoughts and feelings about your losses. Then let the busyness of your thoughts go.

If you find your mind drifting, easily distracted, or struggle to find downtime in your life, try reading Psalm 31, and listen to what God is saying to you there. God speaks to us in his Spirit. The Spirit is activated through the stimulus of truth. Don't be discouraged if you don't hear an audible message from God. He is always speaking to you through his Holy Word.

Sometimes it helps to read aloud or change up your surroundings. Take a walk, sit on the porch, head to the nearest park bench, or simply sit in your car alone for a few minutes if necessary.

Behind the scenes

oss can make you feel hopeless and worthless. Naomi's culture told her that her worth was tied to being a wife and mother of sons, and now she was neither. She had no status in the community and no means of earning a living. She felt hopeless and powerless in her circumstances, and when she decided to return home it was with an attitude to protect and defend herself. Yet she didn't know that the God of hope was already at work.

Hope is wanting something you don't have or wanting something to happen that hasn't happened. Biblical hope is wanting something you can't yet see but can be confident it will come in the future. The Bible spells out the glory we can hope for beyond this life, and that hope is an anchor when life sets our boats adrift. But what can you confidently hope for in this life? Is God at work in your here and now? How?

In this study you will see that God was already working behind the scenes of Naomi's life, long before she saw the fulfillment of things she couldn't bring herself to even hope for. He is working behind the scenes in your life, too. By choosing not to define yourself by your current life circumstances, you can get in on something amazing.

Check In

Before you dive into the video, take a few minutes to check in with each other. Let each person choose one of the following to respond to:

→ What did you get out of the "On Your Own" activities you did for Session 1?

→ Where did you live before the place where you live now? How was it different from the place where you live now? How were you different, or not different?

Next, say your memory verse aloud together. Be sure to say the verse reference after it. If you don't know the verse from memory yet, read it with the group from page 25.

At a Glance: NAOMI

Age-old problem: Feeling of emptiness

Age-old mistake: Losing hope that things can change

God's timeless wisdom: Take action on the things you have the power to influence, and pin your hope on God's never-failing love for the rest. *"But the eyes of the Lord are on those who fear him, on those whose hope is in his unfailing love"* (Psalm 33:18 NIV).

Play the video segment for Session 2. It's about 17 minutes long. As you watch, use the following outline to record thoughts that stand out to you.

DRAMA: *Nicole*

Losing the thing you love more than life itself often reveals your deepest struggle.

TEACHING: *Jada*

Providence: "A timely preparation for future eventualities."

Many times we see God's providence before his provision.

Harvest is not just about the availability of food; it's about the abundance of food.

When you choose to define yourself by your life circumstances, you can miss out on the calling God has for you.

Where am I on this spectrum from pleasant to bitter?

How many divine moments have we missed because we have chosen to define ourselves by our life circumstances?

GOD is working behind the *scenes* in your life, too.

Leader, read each numbered prompt to the group.

1 What stood out to you most from the video?

2 In the drama, the mother whose daughter ran away said, "Losing the thing you love more than life itself often reveals your deepest struggle. Mine was with God. Would I trust God if I couldn't control the outcome?" How do you typically deal with important situations when you can't control the outcome?

3 Naomi looked at her circumstances and wanted to rename herself "Bitter." She was defining herself by her circumstances. What's wrong with doing that?

4   Naomi thought God was against her, but he was working
    in her life in ways she didn't expect and couldn't imagine.
    How does God work in our lives in ways we don't expect?
    Give an example.

5   How easy is it for you to believe that God is at work
    behind the scenes in your life now? What helps you
    believe that? What gets in the way?

6   When Naomi decided to go home to the land where God
    was, God led Naomi to a place of harvest, of abundance.
    What would it mean for you to "go home to the land
    where God is"? (It may or may not be a physical place.)

Select a volunteer

to read the following:

Jada quoted your memory verse:

I am the LORD your God,
who brought you up out of Egypt.
Open wide your mouth, and I will fill it.
(Psalm 81:10 NIV)

Here the psalmist says that just as God freed the Israelites from slavery in Egypt generations ago, so also he can and will satisfy the needs of their descendants in the present day. All we need to do, as he says in the rest of the psalm, is to listen to him and follow his ways. She also quoted the following verse:

May the God of hope fill you with all joy and peace in believing, so that by the power of the Holy Spirit you may abound in hope. (Romans 15:13 ESV)

This passage says God wants to fill us with joy and peace and make us abound in hope. All we need to do is believe him.

7 Complete this sentence with something that you know God has done for you in the past: I am the Lord your God who _____ _____ .

8 To "open wide your mouth" means to ask God. Can you believe that if you ask, God will fill your mouth? If not, what is keeping you from believing it? If you do believe it, what will listening to him and following his ways look like in your case?

In preparation for the coming week, write one thing you want to gain from your study time:

(ex.: hope for my future, a better understanding of who I am...)

Closing Prayer

Ask for a volunteer to read this prayer aloud over the group:

God of heaven and earth, you are the God of the harvest. You are the one who provides for us not just a little but abundantly. Sometimes that's hard for us to believe when we're living through a period of famine, when we feel empty and have no idea where what we need is going to come from. But you are the God who works behind the scenes to bring events together that we can't foresee. Please help us to listen to you, trust you, and follow your ways, and give us the courage to open wide our mouths so that you will fill them. We need your joy, your peace, your hope. We need some very concrete things. Please provide for each one of us. In Jesus' name, amen.

Keep This Close

As you go on your way this week, here are some thoughts from the video that you may want to save in your phone or write on a sticky note so you can refer back to them:

→ "Courage is fear that has said its prayers."—C. S. Lewis
→ When you choose to define yourself by your life circumstances, you can miss out on the calling God has for you.
→ Even before you see things work themselves out, God is working behind the scenes.

On Your Own

Memory Verse

This week, continue to practice saying
aloud your memory verse:

*I am the LORD your God,
who brought you up out of Egypt.
Open wide your mouth and I will fill it.*

(PSALM 81:10 NIV)

In Real Life:

DRAMA: Letting Go

This session's drama is about a mother who found pills in her teenage daughter's backpack. She was overcome by fear and went wild trying to find out whether her daughter was using drugs. She tried to control things about her daughter's life to the point where her daughter eventually ran away. Then the mother learned some crucial things about herself and where to go from there.

1   What, for you, is the equivalent of finding pills in your daughter's backpack? What has upended your world?

2   How are you trying to deal with this? What specific things have you done?

3   When you look at the specifics of what you've done, do you find yourself, like the mom in the drama, trying to

control the outcome? Has fear made you do anything?
If so, what have been the results so far? Think about the
effects on you, on the situation, and on others.

4 When you think about trusting God with this situation,
what goes through your mind?

5 Read Psalm 130. This is another psalm of lament. But in
this case, lament doesn't take up the whole poem. Instead,
the poet spends some time taking his eyes off his circumstances and putting them on God. What does he say that is
definitely lament?

6 What does he tell himself about God?

In verses 5–6, he says what he has decided to do. A little background may help. Watchmen stood on the walls of a city at night, looking out into the wild lands beyond and watching for the stealthy approach of enemies. Because they're up for hours at night and on their feet, with danger constantly on their minds, they passionately wait for morning, when they can get something to eat and go to bed.

7 Why do you suppose waiting for God like this (verses 5–6) is such an important part of a smart response to situations that turn our worlds upside down? How could waiting be so important? What happens when we wait for God? How does waiting affect us?

8 What would waiting for God look like in your current situation? What would you stop doing? What would you keep doing?

Naomi in The Bible

SCRIPTURE ACTIVITY

Look up Ruth chapter 2 and read it.

A little background will help you understand it. First, remember from the end of Ruth, chapter 1 that it is the beginning of the barley harvest. All of the field workers around Bethlehem will go to their bosses' fields and begin harvesting barley. They will cut down the tall stalks of barley and gather them into bundles for transport. They will work as quickly and efficiently as possible, but inevitably in their haste they will leave behind a few stalks, especially at the edges of the fields. A landowner who is most concerned about his profit will then send a worker or two into his field to *glean* it—that is, to carefully cut and gather all of the remaining stalks so that nothing is wasted. But God's law says that instead, landowners should allow the poor people in the neighborhood to glean their fields (Leviticus 23:22). Harvesting barley is hard, backbreaking work, and this law allows the poor who own no land and have no job to do real work and get enough to eat. It is God's law, but there are no police to enforce it, so it depends on social custom and the conscience of the individual landowner.

Naomi and Ruth are poor. As women, they have almost no opportunity to get work. In Ruth 2:2, Ruth offers to go to a field and glean it so they will have barley to eat.

Next, it's helpful to understand why in Ruth 2:8–9 Boaz tells Ruth to keep working in his field and to stay close to his female workers. In that culture, women without men to protect them are extremely vulnerable to sexual assault. Boaz imagines what might happen to Ruth in someone else's field, and he takes steps to protect her.

Finally, in verse 20 Naomi tells Ruth that Boaz *"is a close relative of ours, one of our redeemers" (ESV).* A redeemer in Naomi's culture is a male relative who is expected to take action for a relative in need of justice or help. A redeemer is responsible for avenging a relative's murder, buying his property so that it won't be sold outside the family, and so on.

1 What does God's law about gleaning tell you about God? What is your opinion about it?

2 We don't see much of Naomi in this chapter, but she gives guidance to Ruth in verse 20 What does she say and do? What does this say about her? Could this indicate a change in Naomi's attitude?

3 Jada spoke about providence in this session's video. Where do you see God's providence at work in Ruth chapter 2?

4 How is God already at work addressing Naomi's emptiness and bitterness?

5 Where do you expect the story to go from here?

6 When you think about your own situation, how does this part of Naomi's story affect you?

Journal Time

Choose *one* of the following topics to journal about:

→ Have you been defining yourself by your circumstances? If so, what definition or identity have you been wearing? How has that affected your thoughts, feelings, and actions? How *would* you like to define yourself?

→ Where might God be at work in your life right now behind the scenes? How might he be trying to lead you to a place of harvest? How can you best cooperate with him?

→ Where are you right now on the spectrum from pleasant (5) to bitter (1)? Are you mad at God? Do you feel like he owes you, that he's left you empty? Journal your honest feelings. Then ask yourself how you're going to respond. Are you going to be defined by your current life situation and emotions? Or are you going to ask God if he has something greater in store? Do you believe that even in your hunger and hopeless feelings, the God of the harvest can create a hopeful situation?

Whichever topic you choose, finish up by writing about this question: What will you do differently in your day-to-day life as a result of this reflection? How will this change your conversations, your prayer life, what you say to your friends, how you deal with your problems?

PRAYER ACTIVITY

You understand that you shouldn't define yourself by your circumstances, so how should you define yourself? Your deepest identity is in not how well your life is going, how much money you have, what you do for a living, whether you have children, or what your gender or ethnicity is. Your deepest identity is being a child of God, a member of God's family. You are far from worthless; you are enough as you are because God has made you enough.

Spend some time praying over 1 John 3:1–2 below:

> *See what kind of love the Father has given to us, that we should be called children of God; and so we are. The reason why the world does not know us is that it did not know him. Beloved, we are God's children now, and what we will be has not yet appeared; but we know that when he appears we shall be like him, because we shall see him as he is. (ESV)*

In a private journal, write out a prayer to God, asking him to show you what it looks like to define yourself as his child. What does a child of God desire? What is unimportant to a child of God? What does a child of God fear, and not fear? What makes a child of God feel valuable at the end of the day? How does a child of God deal with other people's expectations? How does a child of God think about circumstances that aren't going so well? Ask God to give you a vivid picture of what your life is about as his child. Ask him to show you how he wants you to deal with your circumstances. When you're ready, write down three things you are thankful for in all of this.

SESSION 3

Better
Than Being
fixed

There are lots of reasons why you may be reluctant to be honest with God and those close to you about your pain, fear, anger, and confusion. You may have been taught that God wants you to *"Rejoice in the Lord always" (Philippians 4:4),* and that sounds like "Lament to the Lord never." You may have been ridiculed or ignored as a child when you cried. Your pain may feel so huge that you can't imagine anyone being able to handle it and continue to respect you as an adult. You may be so angry at God that you don't want to get near him. You may fear that someone will respond to your honesty by trying to fix your emotions and your situation, instead of truly listening to you. All of these are understandable reasons for not being honest, and yet honesty is vital for a life with God.

God's perspective on Naomi's life was that he was providentially working behind the scenes of her life to bring her emptiness to fullness. He had heard her lament, and he was responding. Our human perspective often blinds us to his work and makes us doubt that our lament could make any difference. But as we will hear in this study, we need to know that we have a God we can cry out to even in our confusion, a God who accepts us and tells us the truth about who we really are.

Check In

Before you dive into the video, take a few minutes to check in with each other. Give everyone a chance to respond to the following:

→ What did you get out of the "On Your Own" activities you did for Session 2?

→ When you were a child, what were you taught to do when you were hurt? Or what did you learn to do without being directly taught?

Next, say your memory verse aloud together. Be sure to say the verse reference with it.

At a Glance: NAOMI

Age-old problem: Loss and grief

Age-old mistake: Hide the pain from others and from God

God's timeless wisdom: Let others be drawn to you by the honesty with which you deal with loss in the presence of God.

"As for me, I am poor and needy, but the Lord takes thought for me. You are my help and my deliverer; do not delay, O my God!" (Psalm 40:17 ESV)

Play the video segment for Session 3. It's about 17 minutes long. As you watch, use the following outline to record thoughts that stand out to you.

DRAMA: Nicole

A mom speaks about life after her son has graduated from high school.

I will turn my tassel too. I promise.

TEACHING: Kasey

Trusting God is not going to fix us. It's going to tell us the truth about who we are.

Naomi's God was not trying to fix her. He did not need anything from her.

We will never trust God standing outside the flames.

Are you attractive to other people? Do other people want to be around you because they connect to you, because you openly share your pain with them?

Ruth watched Naomi walk through the fire with a God that Naomi could cry out to, come to, be angry with, be confused by.

Leader, read each numbered prompt to the group.

1 What stood out to you most from the video?

2 Kasey says trusting God is not going to fix us. It's going to tell us the truth about who we are: women accepted by God. What do you think is wrong with wanting God or someone else to fix us?

Select a volunteer to read the following:

Trusting God begins a process of transforming us to become like Jesus in our character (2 Corinthians 3:18). It increasingly improves our ability to treat other people well (Galatians 5:22–23). Also, if we have more trust, we may have less anxiety. And if we deeply believe God accepts us, we will probably feel less shame. But trusting God isn't a quick and automatic solution to unpleasant emotions and relationship difficulties. Nor does it necessarily resolve the problems in our circumstances. So it doesn't necessarily make us feel good. And the change in deeply ingrained habit patterns takes time. Some aspects of our personality may not change in this lifetime. This is what we mean when we say that trusting God doesn't "fix" us.

3 Do you know deeply that you are accepted by God? How does knowing it affect the way you feel about yourself and the way you interact with others? Or how does not knowing it affect how you feel and what you do?

4 How do you think a person gets to know that she is fully, completely accepted by God? Are there things she does or doesn't do? Are there things that happen to her? Are there things that other people do or don't do?

5 Kasey said Naomi had a God she could cry out to, come to, be angry with, be confused by. A God who wasn't trying to fix her. Do you have a God like that? Or do you see God differently? Describe how you see God.

6 Has suffering caused you to focus on yourself and shut others out? Or has it turned your heart to hear the needs in others' cries? Describe how it's done one or the other, or some of each, or something else.

7 What do you think makes the difference between someone getting isolated, bitter, or destructive because of suffering, or someone getting transformed and moved to reach outward to others because of suffering? Are there things other people can do that draw the person in one direction or the other? Are there choices the person makes? Is it something God needs to do that the person receives or doesn't receive?

The change
in deeply ingrained habit patterns takes TIME.

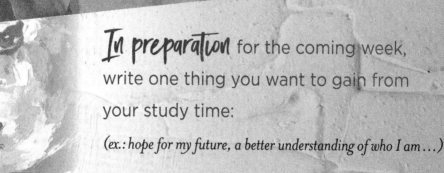

In preparation for the coming week, write one thing you want to gain from your study time:

(ex.: hope for my future, a better understanding of who I am …)

Closing Prayer

Ask for a volunteer to read this prayer aloud over the group:

Creator God, we are so grateful that you have created a place for us to honestly explore these hard questions. Thank you that you are a God we can cry out to, be angry with, and be confused by—and still you are our loving God. A God who totally accepts us the way we are now and isn't trying to fix us so that we "behave." Please be the bedrock Presence in our lives who holds and carries us through seasons of suffering. Please use that suffering to move us out of business as usual and into a life that is offered for the good of others. Please heal in us the harmful effects of past and present suffering that have hardened our hearts in big and small ways. Please give us the courage to move toward others honestly with freedom and joy. We pray this in Jesus' name, amen.

Keep This Close

As you go on your way this week, here are some thoughts from the video that you may want to save in your phone or write on a sticky note so you can refer back to them:

→ Trusting God is going to tell us the truth about who we are.
→ We need a God we can cry out to, come to, be angry with, be confused by. A God who isn't trying to fix us.

On Your Own

Memory Verse

This week, continue to practice saying
aloud your memory verse:

I am the LORD *your God,*
who brought you up out of Egypt.
Open wide your mouth and I will fill it.

(PSALM 81:10 NIV)

In Real Life:

DRAMA ACTIVITY: Turning the Tassel

In the drama, a mom speaks about her feelings after her son has graduated from high school. She refers to the moment when he moved the tassel on his mortarboard from one side to the other.

1 In what ways is the drama a modern-day lament?

2 The mom in the drama talked about "that deep, sinking feeling of being left." Have you ever felt that feeling? If so, what was that like for you?

3 How has that affected who you are today?

4 Read Psalm 22:1–11. This is another psalm of lament, though later it does get around to promising to praise God for deliverance (verses 25–31). But let's not move too quickly to the praise. In verses 1–11, what negative feelings and thoughts does the psalmist express honestly?

5 What does the psalmist remind himself about God (verses 3–5, 9–10)?

6 Does any of what he tells himself about God help you face your own current situation? If so, what?

7 How is this psalm like the way you talk to God? How is it different?

8 What do you want to say to God as a result of this reflection?

Naomi in The Bible

SCRIPTURE ACTIVITY

Read Ruth chapter 3.

Once again, a little knowledge of customs in Naomi's culture will help you follow the story. First, in Ruth 3:2, Naomi says Boaz "is winnowing barley tonight at the threshing floor." Winnowing was a way of separating kernels of grain from dirt and from the papery chaff that encased them. The workers loosened the barley kernels from the straw stalks and spread the kernels on a wide flat area called a threshing floor. Then with winnowing fans they tossed the kernels into the air, and the wind blew away the lighter dirt and chaff. The heavy kernels fell to the ground. A threshing floor was always laid out in an open area where the maximum available wind was likely to blow.

Next, Ruth again calls Boaz a "redeemer" (3:9). One of the responsibilities of a dead man's near relative in this culture is to marry his widow and have a child to carry on his family line. Deuteronomy 25:5–10 says it is the responsibility of the late husband's brother, but Ruth's late husband has no living brother, and the book of Ruth suggests that another near relative has the option of doing the job. He isn't obliged to do it by law, but he can do it as an act of generosity toward his kin. That is what Naomi is hoping for when she sends Ruth to Boaz.

1 What do you think of Naomi's plan in Ruth 3:1–4? What do you think Ruth is risking by doing what Naomi says? Why does Naomi think the risk is worthwhile?

2 When Ruth identifies herself to Boaz in verse 9 and then asks him to act as a redeemer, he says, "May you be blessed by the LORD, my daughter. You have made this last kindness greater than the first in that you have not gone after young men, whether poor or rich" (verse 10 ESV). To whom do you think she is being kind by not going after young men? Why do you think that?

3 If you were to create Boaz's Facebook profile, what would you write?

4 Where do you see God at work behind the scenes in this episode of the story?

5 What can this episode teach us about the ways we cooperate with God in addressing the challenges in our lives?

6 What do you expect will happen in the final episode of this story? Why do you expect that?

Journal Time

Choose *one* of the following topics to journal about:

→ Kasey said, "It is painful saying no to something we have grown to love." What is that thing or person that you have grown to love but that isn't consistent with your best self? What does it give you that motivates you to cling to it? How is it causing harm? What would saying no to it involve? What help do you need to do that?

→ What is suffering doing to you? Who have you become because of this pain? What do you like about who you have become, and/or what don't you like? Who would you like to be? How would you like to affect others? What will it take for you to get there? What help will you need?

→ Are you attractive to other people? Do other people want to be around you because they connect to you, because you openly share your pain and hardship with them? Why do you suppose that's the case? How does that manifest in your life? If you're not a person who other people connect with, what do you think it would take for you to get there?

→ How real is it to you that God fully and totally accepts you? What helps you believe that? What gets in the way? How do you think God sees you? Where did you get that perception? What do you need from God that might help you believe that he fully accepts you?

Whichever topic you choose, finish up by writing about this question: What will you do differently in your day-to-day life as a result of this reflection?

Listening

PRAYER ACTIVITY

Write God a letter expressing your uncensored feelings about him and your current situation. This can be completely from your human perspective without regard for what you think you should be feeling or thinking. If you're in a really positive place, that's great. If you're in a really negative place, remember that's not a problem for God.

Dear God,

Now write some things about God that you know are true, based on what you've read in the Bible or heard taught or experienced for yourself. Write things that are relevant to what you wrote above.

If you can't think of anything, look at the way Psalm 22 alternates between a candid expression of the psalmist's feelings and situation on the one hand, and what he knows about God on the other.

God, I know it's true that you . . .

If you have time, write what you think God might want to say back to you. For ideas, see Hebrews 2:14-18; 4:15-16; 5:7-9; and Psalm 91.

Daughter,

From Bitter to
blessed

We often have a very narrow perspective when we look at our lives. Our attention is consumed by what we feel at the moment and how hard circumstances are crowding in on us. We can't see options for action, or other people's needs, or what God might be doing behind the scenes. Our whole story is us and our pain. That was the case for Naomi at the beginning of the book of Ruth. But Naomi chose not to give up on God, and she chose to care about the needs of Ruth. Now in this final study we will see the harvest of her perseverance.

Like Naomi, we too are part of a much bigger story that God has been telling for millennia, a story about God creating the world, pronouncing it good, then getting involved as it began to go wrong, and reaching out to set it right. We can't see the entire role God wants us to play in his big story, but we can choose to trust him day after day after day. And we can choose to involve ourselves in the needs of other people. As Naomi did this, she went from bitter to blessed, from loneliness to legacy. That beautiful transformation is available for us too.

Check In

Before you dive into the video, take a few minutes to check in with each other. Let each person choose one of the following to respond to:

→ What did you get out of the "On Your Own" activities you did for Session 3?

→ How has someone else been a blessing to you? It could be a recent incident or something that happened a long time ago. Try to limit the story to about one minute.

Next, say your memory verse aloud together, along with its reference.

At a Glance: NAOMI

Age-old problem: Unmet needs

Age-old mistake: Thinking only of yourself and how to get your needs met

God's timeless wisdom: Focus on helping others to get their needs met, and trust that God will meet your needs in the process. *"Give, and it will be given to you. A good measure, pressed down, shaken together and running over, will be poured into your lap. For with the measure you use, it will be measured to you" (Luke 6:38 NIV).*

Play the video segment for Session 4. It's about 19 minutes long. As you watch, use the following outline to record thoughts that stand out to you.

DRAMA: Nicole

The art teacher from Session 1 reflects back on what happened a few weeks after all of her belongings showed up broken in her new home.

TEACHING: Jada

Many times our blessing comes after we have facilitated the blessing of someone else.

God can give you legacy beyond what you expected because it's all about his glory.

You don't need to decide who you are. God decided who you were before you were born.

TEACHING: *Kasey*

God is going to give you an opportunity to serve in the midst of your pain because the surefire antidote to anxiety, isolation, and depression is to serve others.

Choose to trust God over and over and over again until you feel it.

YOU, too, can have the great *reversal.*

Group Discussion

Leader, read each numbered prompt to the group.

1 Is God gathering up the shards of your broken life and making something new? Share something new he has done.

2 Naomi's blessing came after she made an effort to see that Ruth was blessed. How can we facilitate the blessing of someone else? What opportunities do we have?

3 What obstacles do we face in making our lives about helping others?

4 Peter said God's divine power has granted to us all things that pertain to life and godliness (2 Peter 1:3). Yet Peter was then arrested and slowly and brutally executed. His need for physical well-being was taken away. So what did Peter mean when he said that God has granted us all things that pertain to life and godliness?

Select a volunteer to read the following:

Kasey said freedom is abiding in Christ. That's Christian language from the Bible, but what does it mean? First, to abide means to endure, to last a long time. It also means to dwell. Dwelling in connection to Christ is a way of life that we need to begin to practice so that over time it becomes a habit, day after day.

Second, Bible teacher Sinclair Ferguson says, "abiding in Christ means allowing His Word to fill our minds, direct our wills, and transform our affections."[†] It means to bet our lives daily on Jesus' love for us that he displayed on the cross. It means to increasingly love others (with his help) because we love him. It means to trust him moment by moment, especially in hard times, letting the pain strip away everything false and reveal the persons we were meant to be. It means to spend time with Jesus, to drink him in. This is where real satisfaction comes from.

† Sinclair Ferguson, "What Does It Mean to Abide in Christ?" Ligonier Ministries, February 19, 2018, https://www.ligonier.org/blog/what-does-it-mean-abide-christ/.

Spend time with JESUS, drink him in. This is where real *satisfaction* comes from.

5 What is a step of abiding in Christ that you could take in your current situation?

6 Share with the group: What are you grateful for that you've received from this study on Naomi? What will you take with you?

1 Take a minute on your own to write down your response to these questions (you won't have to share your answers):

Think of your emotional and spiritual life like your gas tank. On a scale of 0 to 5, with 0 being empty and 5 being full, how full is your tank today? Mark where you are on the measuring line below.

0	1	2	3	4	5
empty					full

If your tank is not very full, how much *hope* do you have of its being full one day in the future? Can you look forward to a day when things will be a lot better than they are now, or do you see emptiness as far as the horizon? Mark your level of hope on the measuring line below.

0	1	2	3	4	5
no hope					lots of hope

In preparation for the coming week, write one thing you want to gain from your study time:

(ex.: hope for my future, a better understanding of who I am ...):

Closing Prayer

Ask for a volunteer to read this prayer aloud over the group:

Loving God, thank you that you are transforming us from bitter to blessed. Thank you that we can trust you with our circumstances, because we know that when we are not in control—you are. You have already given us everything we need for life and intimacy with you, so help us abide in these things, as they are enough. Continue to tune our hearts to the cries of others so that we might contribute to their transformation and healing. Please keep us connected to you, drawing strength from you every day. Thank you for what you are doing in us, seen and unseen. All of these requests we bring to you in Jesus' name, amen.

keep This Close

As you go on your way this week, here are some thoughts from the video that you may want to save in your phone or write on a sticky note so you can refer back to them:

- → Many times our blessing comes after we have facilitated the blessing of someone else.
- → In our suffering there is a choice. We can choose to trust God over and over and over again.

On Your Own

Memory Verse

Continue to practice saying aloud
your memory verse:

*I am the LORD your God,
who brought you up out of Egypt.
Open wide your mouth and I will fill it.*

(PSALM 81:10 NIV)

In Real Life:

DRAMA ACTIVITY: Broken, Part 2

The art teacher from Session 1 reflects back on a work of art she received as a gift. It was made up of the broken shards of stained glass from her disastrous moving experience. A picture of God's redeeming love.

1 Think of the broken shards of your life that God is shaping into a new work of art. Have you begun to glimpse the new work that God is making? What can you see? What can't you see?

2 How tempted are you, like the art teacher, to throw away all the broken pieces of what has been shattered? What would you miss by doing that?

3 Psalm 40 is a psalm with a lot of celebration and yet still some lament. This poet is grateful for what God has done for him, but he still has real desperation that hasn't been tied up in a bow. In verses 1–3, what has God done for this poet?

4 Read verses 11–17. What is still going on in the poet's life?

5 All of that is still going on in his life, and yet the poet is able to celebrate God. What does this say about his view of his life and of God?

6 In these four sessions we have looked at four approaches to lament, from pure honesty about how bad things are to a mix of gratitude and outcry for help. In a messy and honest spiritual life, we can move back and forth among these. What is most helpful for you in your current state? Offer a prayer to God that expresses where you are right now.

Naomi in The Bible

SCRIPTURE ACTIVITY

Read Ruth chapter 4.

The first scene takes place at the town gate. This was the main entrance to the town, and it was where the elders spent their time and where legal matters were settled. It was a good location for public business because people heading out to their fields or home from their fields had to pass through the gate.

In verses 1–6, the other redeemer isn't named. Israelite tradition won't let him buy Elimelech's land unless he also takes Elimelech's widowed daughter-in-law, Ruth. But Israelite custom will reckon her firstborn son not as the legal son of her new husband, but as the legal son of her late husband. The new husband will pay all the expense of buying the land, feeding Ruth and Naomi, and raising the son, but as soon as the son is an adult, he will inherit Elimelech's land. And if Ruth has more children, the new husband will have to include them as his heirs along with the children he already has. He probably already has a wife and children, and so doesn't want to dilute his estate in this way.

Boaz may have more money than his kinsman, so he can afford to support Ruth, Naomi, and whatever children Ruth may have.

1   How do the events of chapter 4 affect Naomi?

2 In chapter 1, Naomi asked the women of her Bethlehem community to call her "Bitter." Now in 4:14-15, these same women bless the Lord on her behalf and ask a blessing on her and her family. What would you say is the significance of this faith community in her life? Why is the community important?

 Do you have a community that can observe and bless God's work in your life? If so, what difference does that make to you? If not, what difference might it make?

4 Ruth's son became an ancestor of King David (verses 17-21), the greatest of Israel's kings. He also then became an ancestor of Jesus (Matthew 1:1-6). What does this tell you about where Naomi's story fits into the bigger story of the whole Bible?

5 Naomi's story mattered in God's big story far more than she could possibly guess in her lifetime. Your story also matters in God's big story far more than you can see from where you sit. But what *do* you know about where you fit in God's big story of drawing people from all over the world to himself?

6 If you were to dream, what would you like to contribute to God's story?

Journal Time

Here are some journaling topics to consider:

→ What opportunity do you have to pour energy and love into someone else's life? What will that cost you? What do you think about that cost? What will be the benefits of offering yourself in that way? What obstacles do you face in doing that? How could you address those obstacles? How do you respond to the idea of helping others in the midst of what you are going through?

→ How could you abide in Christ this week, day by day? What will that cost you? What will be the benefits? What resistance have you felt in the past when you have tried to take consistent, daily time with God? What resistance have you felt when you have tried to trust God? Do you think you have any unrealistic expectations about what it should feel like to connect with God on a regular basis? If so, what are they? How might God help you get past your resistance and expectations?

→ How has your view of God changed over the course of this study? Who is God to you now? Is God someone you can go to with your pain, anger, confusion? Is he someone you want to be close to? Or do you still have doubts about God?

Whichever topic(s) you choose, finish up by writing about this question: What will you do differently in your day-to-day life as a result of this study?

PRAYER ACTIVITY

Abiding in Christ should be like breathing in and out. We inhale by spending time with God, letting him feed us with his words of encouragement, truth, beauty, and sometimes correction. We tell him everything that's on our minds, so that he can carry it. Then on the exhale, we go out into the world and pour his energy and love into others. We take time to let him meet our needs, and then we take time to give ourselves to others' needs.

Give yourself ten minutes to talk with God about this in-and-out process in your life. What are the parts that come naturally to you? What are the parts that don't? For instance, does reading the Bible feel like work that doesn't feed your soul? If so, ask God to show you what you should be reading and how. Maybe you need to take one scene or one teaching from the Gospel of Luke at a time, and pray over it. Or one verse from a psalm. Is it hard for you to be honest with God in prayer about yourself? Is it hard for you to give some focused attention to praying for someone else, or perhaps you find it hard to put words to what you want to say? Tell God whatever is hard for you, and ask him to help you. Are you find yourself drained in pouring love into someone else, or are you so caught up in your difficulties that pouring love into someone else seems impossible? If so, tell God where you're stuck. Ask him to show you why you're finding yourself so drained, and what you should do about it. If you're overwhelmed, ask him to show you one practical step of love you could take for one person. Whatever your strengths and weaknesses, take them to God and invite him to train you how to breathe him in and breathe out love to others.

About the *Authors*

Jada Edwards, Bible Teacher, Speaker, Author

Jada is an experienced Bible teacher and has committed her life to equipping women of all ages with practical, biblical truth. She currently serves as the Women's Pastor and as the Director of Creative Services for One Community Church in Plano, Texas. Jada teaches a midweek women's Bible study to over 1,300 women each week. She has authored two books based on her Bible studies: *Captive Mind* and *Thirst*. She and her husband, Conway, have a son, Joah, and a daughter, Chloe.

Nicole Johnson, Dramatist and Author

A bestselling author, performer, and motivational speaker, Nicole is one of the most sought-after creative communicators in America today. Her unique ability to blend humor with compassion, as she captures the inner-most feelings of women facing life's daily struggles, has enabled her to create a unique sense of community for women of all ages. Nicole has 20 years' experience as an actor, television host, and producer, and has published eight books and a variety of curricula regarding relationships. She has written and performed sketches for the Women of Faith Conferences and written and directed dramas for The Revolve Tour. For three years, she wrote and performed dramatic sketches with relationship expert Dr. Gary Smalley, bringing her unique perspective to his seminars.

Kasey Van Norman, Author, Bible Teacher, Counselor

Kasey is a bestselling author, licensed counselor, and Bible teacher living in Bryan, Texas with her husband, Justin, and their two children, Emma Grace and Lake. Kasey has published two books and Bible studies, *Named by God* and *Raw Faith*. Kasey teaches and writes about the love that redeemed her life from the shame of past abuse, addiction, infidelity, and the fear of a life-threatening cancer diagnosis. She teaches thousands of women each year as a ministry event speaker—a headliner with the Extraordinary Women Conferences and American Association of Christian Counselors, and as an ambassador with Compassion International.

KNOWN
BY
Name

The women in the Bible asked the same three questions we all still ask today:

How does everyone else see me?

How do I see myself?

How does God see me?

The Known by Name series explores complex women in the Bible and their struggles with tough questions through the lenses of a counselor, a Bible teacher, and a dramatist.

Kasey Van Norman is a bestselling author, licensed counselor, and Bible teacher living in Texas with her husband and their two children. Kasey teaches and writes about the love that redeemed her life from the shame of past abuse, addiction, infidelity, and the fear of a life-threatening cancer diagnosis.

Jada Edwards is an experienced Bible teacher committed to equipping women of all ages with practical, biblical truth. She currently serves as the Women's Pastor and Director of Creative Services for One Community Church in Plano, Texas. She and her husband have two children.

Nicole Johnson, bestselling author, performer, and motivational speaker, is one of the most sought-after creative communicators in America today. She uniquely blends humor with compassion, creating a sense of community for women of all ages. She makes California home with her husband and children.

RAHAB

Don't Judge Me,
God Says I'm

Qualified

Rahab's story, found in the book of Joshua, is a story of a girl boss, an assertive, confident woman who did what she had to do to provide for her family. Her identity was shaped by her upbringing. With no Bible study to join or podcast to download, Rahab learned her behaviors in a culture that believed in gods, not God. But when opportunity knocked, she boldly trusted in God, and became a woman who brought freedom to generations.

This four-session video Bible study will take you through the story of Rahab, our sister in Scripture who trusted God's final word about her worth above society's. Through her story, you will learn how to shed unhelpful labels and fears, and instead revel in God's unconditional love and acceptance of you—just as you are.

HAGAR

In the Face of Rejection,
God Says I'm

Significant

Hagar's story, found in Genesis 16, is a story of cultural victimization. She was betrayed, abandoned, and scorned. Her response? She did what most of us would do when deeply hurt by someone we trust—she ran away. She got defensive. She retreated to a place where she felt safe. She felt justified in her anger and hurt. But deep in her core was a woman who longed to be seen and hoped for redemption.

This four-session video Bible study will take you through the story of Hagar, our sister in Scripture who learns through hurt and rejection that what is unresolved is not unseen by God. Through her story, you will learn how to respond when life doesn't affirm you, but God does.

NAOMI

When I Feel Worthless,
God Says I'm

Enough

Naomi's story, found in the book of Ruth, is a story of lost identity. She lost her husband and her sons, which in her culture left her completely without a home or a means to support herself. She was a Hebrew woman in Moabite territory, alone among strangers. She reacted by letting her circumstances define her. But even in her angry, fearful, rather dramatic season of feeling like the victim, God kept showing his faithfulness.

This four-session video Bible study will take you through the story of Naomi, our sister in Scripture who traveled from comfort and security to despair and bitterness; from hopeless drifting to faithful obedience; from loss to redemption in one short lifetime.

FIND THE *perfect* BIBLE STUDY
for you and your group in 5 MINUTES *or* LESS!

Find the right study for your women's group
by answering four easy questions:

1. WHAT TYPE OF STUDY DO YOU WANT TO DO?

- *Book of the Bible:* Dive deep into the study of a Bible character, or go through a complete book of the Bible systematically, or add tools to your Bible study methods toolkit.

- *Topical Issues:* Have a need in a specific area of life? Study the Scriptures that pertain to that need. Topics include prayer, joy, purpose, balance, identity in Christ, and more.

2. WHAT LEVEL OF TIME COMMITMENT BETWEEN SESSIONS WOULD YOU LIKE?

- *None:* No personal homework
- *Minimal:* Less than 30 minutes of homework
- *Moderate:* 30 minutes to one hour of homework
- *Substantial:* An hour or more of homework

3. WHAT IS YOUR GROUP'S BIBLE KNOWLEDGE?

- *Beginner:* Group is comprised mostly of women who are new to the Bible or who don't feel confident in their Bible knowledge.

- *Intermediate:* Group has some experience with studying the Bible, and they have some familiarity with the stories in the Bible.

- *Advanced:* Group is comfortable with the Bible, and can handle the challenge of searching the Scriptures for themselves.

4. WHAT FORMAT DO YOU PREFER?

- *Print and Video:* Watch a Bible teacher on video, followed by a facilitated discussion.
- *Print Only:* Have the group leader give a short talk and lead a discussion of a study guide or a book.

Get Started!

Plug your answers into the **Bible Study Finder**, and discover the studies that best fit your group!

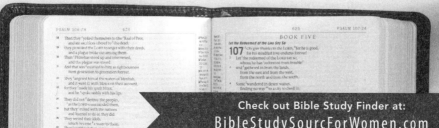

Check out Bible Study Finder at:
BibleStudySourcForWomen.com

.